Our Lady of Good Health Novena

Healing Testimonies, History, Special Prayers, and A Nine-Day Healing and Restoration Prayers

OLIVIA ANDERSON

Contents

Personal Stories of Healing

Mabel's Journey to Health

I've had migraines for as long as I can remember. Those awful headaches felt like someone was driving nails into my skull. I tried everything—prescriptions, holistic remedies, and even some out-there stuff like acupuncture. But nothing worked. One day, a friend, seeing how desperate I was, suggested I pray to Our Lady of Good Health. I was skeptical— how could prayer succeed where medicine had failed? But I was willing to try anything.

I started a novena, a nine-day prayer, and by the third day, I felt this warm sensation in my head during my prayers. It was like a soothing balm, something I had never felt before. Miraculously, my migraines started to diminish, and by the end of the novena, they were completely gone. I haven't had a headache since. I know in my heart it was Our Lady who healed me.

Thomas' Recovery from a Car Accident

The accident was devastating. One minute I was driving home, the next I was in a hospital bed with multiple fractures and the grim news that I might never walk again. It was like my world crumbled in an instant. My family, devout Catholics, insisted on starting a novena to Our Lady of Good Health. I went along with it, mostly to appease them, but I wasn't very hopeful.

On the seventh day of the novena, something incredible happened. I felt a surge of strength I hadn't felt since before the accident. It wasn't just in my body; it was in my spirit too. Against all odds and to the astonishment of my doctors, my recovery accelerated. Within months, I was not only walking but running. There's no other explanation—I was given a miracle by Our Lady of Good Health.

Emily's Healing from Depression

Depression had been my constant companion for years. I felt like I was drowning in darkness with no way out. There were days I didn't want to get out of bed, and I even thought about ending it all. One day, I ran into a nun who seemed to sense my pain. She suggested I start a novena to Our Lady of Good Health. I didn't have much faith, but I was desperate enough to try anything.

As I prayed each day, I began to feel a sense of peace that I hadn't felt in years. It was subtle at first, but by the end of the novena, it was like a heavy fog had lifted. My depression didn't vanish overnight, but I found the strength and clarity to seek help and rebuild my life. I truly believe Our Lady was guiding me toward healing and hope.

Robert's Cure from Cancer

When I was diagnosed with stage four cancer, it felt like a death sentence. The doctors gave me months to live, and all treatments seemed to fail. My wife, a woman of strong faith, started a novena to Our Lady of Good Health. I joined her, but honestly, I had little hope.

On the ninth day of the novena, I went in for a routine check-up. To everyone's astonishment, the scans showed no trace of cancer. The doctors couldn't explain it—it was a complete remission. I am convinced that Our Lady of Good Health granted me a miracle, giving me a new lease on life.

Sarah's Battle with Infertility

For years, my husband and I struggled to conceive. It was heartbreaking to see negative test after negative test. We tried everything, from fertility treatments to alternative therapies, but nothing worked. One day, a friend suggested we pray a novena to Our Lady of Good Health. I was skeptical but willing to give it a shot.

We began the novena together, and just a month later, I found out I was pregnant. It was like a dream come true. We now have a beautiful baby girl, whom we named Mary in honor of the Virgin Mary. I truly believe it was the power of our prayers that brought her to us.

Michael's Escape from Addiction

Addiction had me in its grip for over a decade. I lost my job, my family, and my self-respect. It felt like there was no way out. During a rehab session, a priest suggested I turn to Our Lady of Good Health. I was at rock bottom and willing to try anything, so I started a novena.

By the end of the novena, something changed inside me. I experienced a spiritual awakening that gave me the strength to fight my addiction. I am now clean and have rebuilt my life, thanks to the intercession of Our Lady of Good Health. Her guidance and support were the turning points in my darkest times.

The Healing of Lucia

My daughter Lucia was diagnosed with a rare, incurable disease that left her bedridden. As a parent, it was devastating to watch her suffer. We decided to take her to the shrine of Our Lady of Good Health, praying for a miracle. During our pilgrimage, Lucia's condition seemed to get worse, and I feared we were losing her.

However, as we prayed fervently at the shrine, something incredible happened. Lucia, who had been unable to walk for months, suddenly stood up and began to walk. It was nothing short of a miracle. Her doctors later confirmed that she was completely healed. We believe it was the divine intervention of Our Lady of Good Health that saved our daughter.

Pedro's Recovery from Blindness

I was born blind, and my parents never gave up hope that I might see one day. They made a pilgrimage to the shrine of Our Lady of Good Health when I was ten, praying for a miracle. I remember feeling the intense devotion and hope around me, even though I couldn't see it.

On the final day of our novena, something extraordinary happened. I opened my eyes and saw light for the first time. The shapes and colors were overwhelming, but I knew I was seeing. My family and everyone at the shrine were in tears of joy. It was a miracle, plain and simple, and I am forever grateful to Our Lady of Good Health.

Anna's Lifesaving Operation

When I was diagnosed with a severe heart condition, the doctors said I needed immediate surgery, but the risks were high. The night before my operation, my family gathered around my hospital bed and started a novena to Our Lady of Good Health. We were all nervous but hopeful.

During the surgery, there was a complication that almost cost me my life. The doctors later told us that it felt like an unseen hand guided them through the critical moment, allowing them to successfully complete the surgery. I made a full recovery, and we all believe it was the intervention of Our Lady of Good Health that saved me.

David's Protection During a Storm

As a fisherman, I've faced many storms, but this one was the worst. The waves were like mountains, and I thought I wouldn't make it home. Desperate, I started praying to Our Lady of Good Health, asking for her protection.

Suddenly, the storm began to calm. The waves subsided, and I was able to navigate my boat safely back to shore. I am convinced it was a miracle. The storm's sudden calming felt like a direct response to my prayers. I've shared this story many times, and every time I do, it strengthens my faith and the faith of those who hear it.

Elise's Escape from Danger

One night, as I was walking home, I was confronted by a man who seemed intent on harming me. Terrified, I prayed to Our Lady of Good Health for protection. To my astonishment, the man suddenly turned and fled, as if he had seen something that scared him away.

I was left unharmed and deeply shaken but grateful. I believe Our Lady of Good Health intervened to save me that night. Since then, I've carried a deep faith in her protective power and share my story to remind others that we are never truly alone.

Gabriel's Unexpected Blessing

As an artist, my life was a constant struggle to make ends meet. I was facing financial ruin and felt like giving up. In my desperation, I started a novena to Our Lady of Good Health, praying for a miracle. On the ninth day, I received an unexpected call from a wealthy patron who wanted to sponsor my work.

This turn of events changed my life. I went from the brink of bankruptcy to a successful career, all thanks to the timely intervention I believe was orchestrated by Our Lady of Good Health. Her blessing came at my darkest hour, and I am eternally grateful.

Jessica's Triumph Over Chronic Pain

Living with fibromyalgia was like having an invisible enemy constantly attacking my body. The chronic pain was unbearable, and no treatment seemed to help. A friend suggested I try a novena to Our Lady of Good Health. I was hesitant but desperate enough to try anything.

I started the novena, and by the seventh day, something amazing happened. The pain, which had been my constant companion, started to lessen. By the end of the novena, it was gone. I couldn't believe it. I felt like I had my life back. Now, I lead a support group for people with chronic pain, sharing my story and spreading hope.

Reflections on Faith and Healing

Reflecting on the profound testimonies of healing attributed to Our Lady of Good Health, we find ourselves drawn into a deeper understanding of faith and the miraculous. These stories not only inspire but also challenge us to examine our own spiritual lives and the ways in which we open ourselves to divine intervention. The concept of faith, especially in the Catholic tradition, is not just about belief in doctrines or participation in rituals, but a profound trust in God's presence and power in our lives. This trust is the bedrock upon which miraculous healings and transformations occur.

The testimonies of Mabel, Thomas, Emily, Robert, Sarah, Michael, Lucia, Pedro, Anna, David, Elise, Gabriel, and Jessica serve as beacons of hope. Each story is unique, yet they all share a common thread: the individuals involved turned to Our Lady of Good Health with unwavering faith during their times of need. Their prayers were answered in ways that defy human understanding, illuminating the boundless compassion and intercessory power of the Virgin Mary.

Faith is often described as a journey, one that involves not just the mind but the heart and soul. In these testimonies, we see individuals who, despite their doubts and struggles, embarked on this journey with sincere hearts. Their stories remind us that faith is not about having all the answers or never experiencing doubt. Instead, it is about trusting in God's goodness and mercy, even when circumstances seem dire. This kind of faith opens the door to miracles.

The act of praying a novena, as demonstrated by these testimonies, is a powerful expression of faith. A novena, which consists of nine days of prayer, reflects perseverance and dedication. It is a time of focused prayer, reflection, and trust in God's timing and will. Through this practice, individuals demonstrate their commitment to seeking divine assistance, believing that God hears and answers their prayers. This ritual of sustained prayer is a testament to the Catholic understanding of persistent and hopeful supplication.

In reflecting on these stories, we are reminded of the biblical accounts of healing and miracles. Jesus often said, "Your faith has healed you," emphasizing the crucial role of faith in receiving divine healing. The testimonies of healing through the intercession of Our Lady of Good Health echo this biblical principle. They remind us that faith is not just about believing in the possibility of miracles, but also about actively seeking them through prayer and trust in God's power.

The communal aspect of these stories is also significant. Many of the individuals were supported by their families, friends, or parish communities. This communal prayer and support amplify the power of individual prayers. In Catholic tradition, the community is a vital component of faith life. When we gather in prayer, our collective faith and intercession become a potent force. This is why novenas and other communal prayers hold a special place in Catholic practice. They unite us in our petitions and create a spiritual solidarity that strengthens our individual faith.

Healing, whether physical, emotional, or spiritual, is a profound manifestation of God's love and mercy. In these testimonies, we see various forms of healing: relief from chronic pain, recovery from severe illness, liberation from addiction, and restoration of peace and purpose. Each form of healing is a sign of God's intimate involvement in our lives. It is a reminder that God cares deeply about our well-being and desires to restore us to wholeness.

As we reflect on these miracles, we are invited to deepen our own faith and openness to God's healing power. This involves not only praying for our own needs but also interceding for others. The stories remind us of the importance of praying with intention, specificity, and trust. When we pray for healing, we are not merely asking for a change in our circumstances but inviting God's transformative presence into our lives. This kind of prayer requires humility, acknowledging our dependence on God, and a willingness to surrender to His will.

Moreover, these testimonies challenge us to cultivate a hopeful and expectant faith. It is easy to become discouraged when prayers seem unanswered or when we face prolonged suffering. However, the stories of miraculous healings encourage us to remain hopeful. They remind us that God's timing and ways are often beyond our understanding. What may seem like a delay or a "no" could be God's preparation for a greater blessing or a different form of healing than we anticipated.

In the Catholic tradition, the sacraments play a crucial role in nurturing our faith and preparing us for God's healing. The sacraments of Reconciliation and the Anointing of the Sick, in particular, offer profound encounters with God's mercy and healing. Regular participation in the Eucharist also strengthens our faith, as we receive the Body and Blood of Christ, who is the ultimate healer of our souls and bodies.

The stories of healing through Our Lady of Good Health also invite us to deepen our devotion to the Blessed Virgin Mary. Mary, as the Mother of Jesus and our spiritual mother, holds a special place in Catholic devotion. Her intercessory role is a powerful source of comfort and hope for believers. By turning to Mary in our times of need, we are not only seeking her intercession but also imitating her own faith and trust in God. Mary's life, marked by her fiat—her "yes" to God's will—serves as a model for our own lives of faith.

As we prepare ourselves to receive our own miracles, we are encouraged to approach prayer with a heart full of faith, hope, and love. We are called to trust in God's infinite wisdom and mercy, even when we do not understand His ways. The stories we have reflected upon show us that miracles do happen, often in the most unexpected ways. They inspire us to keep praying, keep believing, and keep hoping, knowing that God's love for us is boundless and His desire to heal us is profound.

Finally, the testimonies of healing attributed to Our Lady of Good Health offer us a powerful reflection on faith and healing. They remind us that faith is an active, living trust in God's presence and power in our lives. Through persistent prayer, communal support, and a hopeful heart, we open ourselves to God's miraculous interventions. As we reflect on these stories, let us be inspired to deepen our own faith, to pray with perseverance, and to trust in God's infinite love and mercy. May Our Lady of Good Health intercede for us, bringing healing and restoration to our lives and the lives of those we love.

Origins and Traditions

The devotion to Our Lady of Good Health, often referred to as Our Lady of Vailankanni, is a deep-rooted and cherished aspect of Catholic tradition, particularly in India. This devotion has origins that blend history, faith, and cultural integration, creating a rich tapestry of belief and practice.

The title "Our Lady of Good Health" refers to the Virgin Mary, the mother of Jesus Christ, revered in Christianity for her purity, obedience to God's will, and her maternal intercession. The origins of this specific devotion are linked to a series of events that took place in the small coastal town of Vailankanni, located in the state of Tamil Nadu, India.

The tradition dates back to the 16th century. According to local lore, there were three significant apparitions of the Virgin Mary in Vailankanni. These apparitions were to a shepherd boy, a poor widow, and a Portuguese merchant. Each apparition was marked by a miraculous event, which firmly established Vailankanni as a sacred site.

The first apparition is said to have occurred in the mid-16th century. A young shepherd boy, suffering from a high fever, was lying under a banyan tree near a pond in Vailankanni. Suddenly, he saw a beautiful lady holding a child in her arms. She asked him for milk for her son. Despite his illness, the boy obliged and gave her the milk. Miraculously, his fever was cured immediately. This event marked the beginning of the devotion to Our Lady of Good Health. The spot where the apparition occurred is now the site of the Basilica of Our Lady of Good Health.

The second apparition took place a few years later. A poor widow and her son made their living by selling buttermilk. One day, as they were resting under the same banyan tree, the Virgin Mary appeared to them and asked for buttermilk for her child. They gladly gave her the buttermilk. She then instructed them to go to Nagapattinam and tell the Catholic priest there about her appearance. The widow and her son did as they were told, and the priest, recognizing the significance of the apparition, initiated the construction of a small thatched chapel at the site. This event further solidified the town's association with miraculous healings and divine intervention.

The third significant event involved a group of Portuguese merchants. According to tradition, in the late 16th century, a Portuguese ship sailing from Macau to Ceylon (Sri Lanka) encountered a violent storm. The terrified sailors, fearing for their lives, prayed fervently to the Blessed Virgin Mary for deliverance. Their prayers were answered as the storm subsided, and they safely reached the shores of Vailankanni on September 8, the feast day of the Nativity of Mary. In gratitude, they built a chapel dedicated to Our Lady of Good Health, marking the site with a permanent structure that would grow in prominence over the centuries.

These origins are more than mere stories; they have been embraced by the faithful, forming the foundation of a living tradition. The belief in the Virgin Mary's intercession for health and well-being has drawn countless pilgrims to Vailankanni, transforming the town into one of the most important Marian shrines in the world. The tradition is not limited to Catholics; people of various faiths come to seek the blessings of Our Lady of Good Health.

Traditionally, devotees participate in novenas, special prayers, and processions, especially leading up to the feast day on September 8. This period is marked by intense religious activities, including masses, recitation of the rosary, and the veneration of statues and icons of Our Lady of Good Health. The novena is a nine-day period of prayer and reflection, asking for the Virgin Mary's intercession in matters of health and personal petitions. It is a practice deeply ingrained in the lives of the devotees, symbolizing their faith and trust in the maternal care of Mary.

In addition to these religious practices, the devotion to Our Lady of Good Health has fostered a range of cultural traditions. Pilgrims often make vows, promising to perform certain acts of piety or charity in exchange for favors received. These acts might include walking barefoot to the shrine, fasting, or offering symbolic items like candles, flowers, or even crutches and wheelchairs, which are left behind by those who believe they have been healed.

The symbolism associated with Our Lady of Good Health is rich and varied. Statues and images of her often depict her in a resplendent gown, holding the infant Jesus, signifying her role as the mother of the divine healer. The infant Jesus is shown with outstretched arms, inviting all to seek his blessings through the intercession of his mother. This imagery is a powerful representation of the theological belief in Mary's role as an intercessor and a source of comfort and healing.

The traditions surrounding Our Lady of Good Health extend beyond the religious realm, influencing social and communal life. The annual feast day celebrations in Vailankanni attract millions of pilgrims from all over the world. This influx of devotees transforms the small town into a bustling center of activity, with makeshift accommodations, food stalls, and vendors selling religious items. The communal aspect of these celebrations fosters a sense of unity and shared faith, transcending geographical and cultural boundaries.

In conclusion, the origins and traditions of the devotion to Our Lady of Good Health are deeply intertwined with history, faith, and cultural practices. From the miraculous apparitions in Vailankanni to the enduring traditions of prayer, pilgrimage, and communal celebration, this devotion continues to inspire and uplift countless believers. It is a testament to the enduring power of faith and the maternal care of the Virgin Mary, providing hope and healing to those who seek her intercession.

Historical Background

The historical background of Our Lady of Good Health is a fascinating journey that spans centuries, involving miraculous events, cultural integration, and the establishment of a major Marian shrine. Understanding this background provides a deeper appreciation of the devotion and its significance in the lives of millions of believers.

The story begins in the 16th century in the small coastal town of Vailankanni, located in the Tamil Nadu state of India. This period was marked by significant Portuguese influence in the region, as they established trade routes and settlements along the Indian coast. The Portuguese, being devout Catholics, played a crucial role in spreading Christianity in the region and establishing places of worship.

The first recorded apparition of Our Lady of Good Health occurred in the mid-16th century. A young shepherd boy, tending to his flock near a pond in Vailankanni, experienced a miraculous vision of the Virgin Mary holding the infant Jesus. According to tradition, the boy was suffering from a high fever, and the apparition of Mary asking for milk for her child resulted in his immediate healing. This event was the genesis of the devotion to Our Lady of Good Health. The spot where this apparition took place is now marked by a basilica, which stands as a testament to the enduring faith of the local community and pilgrims worldwide.

A few years later, the Virgin Mary appeared again, this time to a poor widow and her son who were selling buttermilk. Mary requested buttermilk for her child and instructed them to inform the Catholic priest in Nagapattinam about her appearance. This led to the construction III elevated the church to the status of a basilica, recognizing its importance as a major Marian shrine. This recognition brought international attention to Vailankanni, further boosting the influx of pilgrims and solidifying its status as the "Lourdes of the East."The basilica itself is a striking example of Gothic architecture, with its tall spires, stained glass windows, and spacious interiors designed to accommodate large numbers of worshippers. The statue of Our Lady of Good Health, adorned in regal attire, is the focal point of the basilica, drawing the faithful to seek her intercession. The interior of the basilica is adorned with numerous votive offerings from pilgrims who have experienced miraculous healings, ranging from crutches and wheelchairs to silver and gold replicas of body parts.One of the unique aspects of the Vailankanni shrine is its inclusivity and openness to people of all faiths. Hindu, Muslim, and Christian pilgrims alike come to seek the blessings of Our Lady of Good Health. This interfaith appeal is a testament to the universal nature of Mary's maternal care and the shared human experience of seeking healing and comfort in times of distress.The historical background of Our Lady of Good Health also includes the contributions of various religious orders and missionaries who have served the shrine over the centuries. These dedicated individuals have played a vital role in the pastoral care of pilgrims, the maintenance and expansion of the shrine's facilities, and the promotion of devotion to Our Lady of Good Health. Their tireless efforts have ensured that the shrine remains a vibrant center of faith and devotion.In recent years, the Vailankanni shrine has continued to evolve to meet the needs of modern pilgrims. The infrastructure has been enhanced to accommodate the growing number of visitors, including the construction of guesthouses, medical facilities, and various amenities. The shrine has also embraced modern communication technologies, providing online services for those unable to physically visit, thus extending its reach to a global audience.The historical background of Our Lady of Good Health is not just a story of past events but a living tradition that continues to inspire and transform lives. The miraculous apparitions, the faith and dedication of early devotees, the cultural integration, and the ongoing pastoral care all contribute to the rich tapestry of this devotion. As we reflect on this history, we are reminded of the enduring power of faith, the intercessory role of the Virgin Mary, and the universal human quest for healing and comfort.

Special Prayers

Traditional Prayers to Our Lady of Good Health

Prayer for Guidance and Healing

O Mary, Our Lady of Good Health, loving Mother, and healer of all who seek your intercession, we come before you with open hearts, asking for your guidance and healing touch. You who have shown us the way through your apparitions and miraculous deeds, look upon us with compassion and mercy.

In our moments of weakness and despair, be our strength and comfort. Help us to trust in your maternal care and the infinite love of your Son, Jesus Christ. Guide us in our journey of faith, that we may always walk in the light of your grace and wisdom. We place our lives in your hands, O Mother, knowing that you will lead us to the path of peace and healing. Amen.

Prayer for Strength and Protection

O Blessed Virgin Mary, Our Lady of Good Health, you are the refuge of the weak and the protector of the vulnerable. We turn to you in our time of need, seeking your powerful intercession and protection. Shelter us under your mantle of love and keep us safe from all harm.

Grant us the strength to face the challenges and trials of life with courage and faith. Help us to remain steadfast in our devotion to your Son, even in the face of adversity. May your presence be a constant source of hope and reassurance, guiding us through the storms of life. We entrust ourselves to your loving care, O Mother, and ask for your continued protection. Amen.

Prayer for Peace and Consolation

O Mary, Our Lady of Good Health,
Queen of Peace, we come to you seeking
consolation and inner peace. In the
quiet of your presence, we find comfort
and rest for our weary souls. You who
have experienced the joys and sorrows
of life, understand our struggles and
pain.

Help us to find solace in your maternal
embrace and the assurance of your love.
Grant us the grace to forgive and to be
forgiven, to heal and to be healed.
Amen.

Novena Prayers

Day 1

O Blessed Virgin Mary, Our Lady of Good Health, I come before you today with a heart full of faith and trust. You, who have shown your loving care to countless souls through miraculous healings and answered prayers, I seek your powerful intercession.

Mother of Mercy, I present my special intention to you (mention your special prayer request). You know the depth of my need and the desires of my heart. In your kindness and compassion, please intercede for me with your Son, Jesus, and ask Him to grant me the grace and healing I so fervently seek.

O Mother, I am weary and in need of your strength. My body, mind, and spirit are troubled, and I turn to you for comfort and relief. Just as you healed the sick and comforted the sorrowful, please touch me with your healing hands and restore me to health and peace. Help me to bear my trials with patience and trust in God's plan for me.

Our Lady of Good Health, you have been a beacon of hope for those in distress. I ask you to guide me through the challenges I face, and grant me the courage to persevere in faith. Teach me to place my trust in God, and to find solace in His love and mercy.

O Loving Mother, I pray for the grace to accept God's will in my life, whether it brings healing or continued suffering. Help me to unite my pain with the sufferings of Jesus, and to offer my trials for the salvation of souls. Give me the strength to endure with hope and joy, knowing that your maternal care surrounds me always.

Mary, Health of the Sick, be with me in my moments of weakness and doubt. Grant me the inner peace and serenity that comes from knowing you are by my side. Help me to remain steadfast in prayer, and to trust that God hears my pleas and will answer them in His perfect time.

Thank you for hearing my prayer and for your unwavering love. With confidence, I place myself under your protective mantle, knowing that you will never abandon me.In your holy name, I pray. Amen.

Day 2

O Blessed Virgin Mary, Our Lady of
Good Health, I come before you today
with a heart full of faith and trust. You,
who have shown your loving care to
countless souls through miraculous
healings and answered prayers, I seek
your powerful intercession.

Mother of Mercy, I present my special
intention to you (mention your special
prayer request). You know the depth of
my need and the desires of my heart. In
your kindness and compassion, please
intercede for me with your Son, Jesus,
and ask Him to grant me the grace and
healing I so fervently seek.

O Mother, I am weary and in need of
your strength. My body, mind, and spirit
are troubled, and I turn to you for
comfort and relief. Just as you healed
the sick and comforted the sorrowful,
please touch me with your healing hands

and restore me to health and peace. Help me to bear my trials with patience and trust in God's plan for me.

Our Lady of Good Health, you have been a beacon of hope for those in distress. I ask you to guide me through the challenges I face, and grant me the courage to persevere in faith. Teach me to place my trust in God, and to find solace in His love and mercy.

O Loving Mother, I pray for the grace to accept God's will in my life, whether it brings healing or continued suffering. Help me to unite my pain with the sufferings of Jesus, and to offer my trials for the salvation of souls. Give me the strength to endure with hope and joy, knowing that your maternal care surrounds me always.

Mary, Health of the Sick, be with me in my moments of weakness and doubt. Grant me the inner peace and serenity

that comes from knowing you are by my side. Help me to remain steadfast in prayer, and to trust that God hears my pleas and will answer them in His perfect time.

Thank you for hearing my prayer and for your unwavering love. With confidence, I place myself under your protective mantle, knowing that you will never abandon me.In your holy name, I pray. Amen.

Day 3

O Blessed Virgin Mary, Our Lady of
Good Health, I come before you today
with a heart full of faith and trust. You,
who have shown your loving care to
countless souls through miraculous
healings and answered prayers, I seek
your powerful intercession.

Mother of Mercy, I present my special
intention to you (mention your special
prayer request). You know the depth of
my need and the desires of my heart. In
your kindness and compassion, please
intercede for me with your Son, Jesus,
and ask Him to grant me the grace and
healing I so fervently seek.

O Mother, I am weary and in need of
your strength. My body, mind, and spirit
are troubled, and I turn to you for
comfort and relief. Just as you healed
the sick and comforted the sorrowful,
please touch me with your healing hands

and restore me to health and peace.
Help me to bear my trials with patience
and trust in God's plan for me.

Our Lady of Good Health, you have been
a beacon of hope for those in distress. I
ask you to guide me through the
challenges I face, and grant me the
courage to persevere in faith. Teach me
to place my trust in God, and to find
solace in His love and mercy.

O Loving Mother, I pray for the grace to
accept God's will in my life, whether it
brings healing or continued suffering.
Help me to unite my pain with the
sufferings of Jesus, and to offer my trials
for the salvation of souls. Give me the
strength to endure with hope and joy,
knowing that your maternal care
surrounds me always.

Mary, Health of the Sick, be with me in
my moments of weakness and doubt.
Grant me the inner peace and serenity

that comes from knowing you are by my side. Help me to remain steadfast in prayer, and to trust that God hears my pleas and will answer them in His perfect time.

Thank you for hearing my prayer and for your unwavering love. With confidence, I place myself under your protective mantle, knowing that you will never abandon me.In your holy name, I pray. Amen.

Day 4

O Blessed Virgin Mary, Our Lady of Good Health, I come before you today with a heart full of faith and trust. You, who have shown your loving care to countless souls through miraculous healings and answered prayers, I seek your powerful intercession.

Mother of Mercy, I present my special intention to you (mention your special prayer request). You know the depth of my need and the desires of my heart. In your kindness and compassion, please intercede for me with your Son, Jesus, and ask Him to grant me the grace and healing I so fervently seek.

O Mother, I am weary and in need of your strength. My body, mind, and spirit are troubled, and I turn to you for comfort and relief. Just as you healed the sick and comforted the sorrowful, please touch me with your healing hands

and restore me to health and peace. Help me to bear my trials with patience and trust in God's plan for me.

Our Lady of Good Health, you have been a beacon of hope for those in distress. I ask you to guide me through the challenges I face, and grant me the courage to persevere in faith. Teach me to place my trust in God, and to find solace in His love and mercy.

O Loving Mother, I pray for the grace to accept God's will in my life, whether it brings healing or continued suffering. Help me to unite my pain with the sufferings of Jesus, and to offer my trials for the salvation of souls. Give me the strength to endure with hope and joy, knowing that your maternal care surrounds me always.

Mary, Health of the Sick, be with me in my moments of weakness and doubt. Grant me the inner peace and serenity

that comes from knowing you are by my side. Help me to remain steadfast in prayer, and to trust that God hears my pleas and will answer them in His perfect time.

Thank you for hearing my prayer and for your unwavering love. With confidence, I place myself under your protective mantle, knowing that you will never abandon me.In your holy name, I pray. Amen.

Day 5

O Blessed Virgin Mary, Our Lady of
Good Health, I come before you today
with a heart full of faith and trust. You,
who have shown your loving care to
countless souls through miraculous
healings and answered prayers, I seek
your powerful intercession.

Mother of Mercy, I present my special
intention to you (mention your special
prayer request). You know the depth of
my need and the desires of my heart. In
your kindness and compassion, please
intercede for me with your Son, Jesus,
and ask Him to grant me the grace and
healing I so fervently seek.

O Mother, I am weary and in need of
your strength. My body, mind, and spirit
are troubled, and I turn to you for
comfort and relief. Just as you healed
the sick and comforted the sorrowful,
please touch me with your healing hands

and restore me to health and peace.
Help me to bear my trials with patience
and trust in God's plan for me.

Our Lady of Good Health, you have been
a beacon of hope for those in distress. I
ask you to guide me through the
challenges I face, and grant me the
courage to persevere in faith. Teach me
to place my trust in God, and to find
solace in His love and mercy.

O Loving Mother, I pray for the grace to
accept God's will in my life, whether it
brings healing or continued suffering.
Help me to unite my pain with the
sufferings of Jesus, and to offer my trials
for the salvation of souls. Give me the
strength to endure with hope and joy,
knowing that your maternal care
surrounds me always.

Mary, Health of the Sick, be with me in
my moments of weakness and doubt.
Grant me the inner peace and serenity

that comes from knowing you are by my side. Help me to remain steadfast in prayer, and to trust that God hears my pleas and will answer them in His perfect time.

Thank you for hearing my prayer and for your unwavering love. With confidence, I place myself under your protective mantle, knowing that you will never abandon me.In your holy name, I pray. Amen.

Day 6

O Blessed Virgin Mary, Our Lady of Good Health, I come before you today with a heart full of faith and trust. You, who have shown your loving care to countless souls through miraculous healings and answered prayers, I seek your powerful intercession.

Mother of Mercy, I present my special intention to you (mention your special prayer request). You know the depth of my need and the desires of my heart. In your kindness and compassion, please intercede for me with your Son, Jesus, and ask Him to grant me the grace and healing I so fervently seek.

O Mother, I am weary and in need of your strength. My body, mind, and spirit are troubled, and I turn to you for comfort and relief. Just as you healed the sick and comforted the sorrowful, please touch me with your healing hands

and restore me to health and peace.
Help me to bear my trials with patience
and trust in God's plan for me.

Our Lady of Good Health, you have been
a beacon of hope for those in distress. I
ask you to guide me through the
challenges I face, and grant me the
courage to persevere in faith. Teach me
to place my trust in God, and to find
solace in His love and mercy.

O Loving Mother, I pray for the grace to
accept God's will in my life, whether it
brings healing or continued suffering.
Help me to unite my pain with the
sufferings of Jesus, and to offer my trials
for the salvation of souls. Give me the
strength to endure with hope and joy,
knowing that your maternal care
surrounds me always.

Mary, Health of the Sick, be with me in
my moments of weakness and doubt.
Grant me the inner peace and serenity

that comes from knowing you are by my side. Help me to remain steadfast in prayer, and to trust that God hears my pleas and will answer them in His perfect time.

Thank you for hearing my prayer and for your unwavering love. With confidence, I place myself under your protective mantle, knowing that you will never abandon me.In your holy name, I pray. Amen.

Day 7

O Blessed Virgin Mary, Our Lady of
Good Health, I come before you today
with a heart full of faith and trust. You,
who have shown your loving care to
countless souls through miraculous
healings and answered prayers, I seek
your powerful intercession.

Mother of Mercy, I present my special
intention to you (mention your special
prayer request). You know the depth of
my need and the desires of my heart. In
your kindness and compassion, please
intercede for me with your Son, Jesus,
and ask Him to grant me the grace and
healing I so fervently seek.

O Mother, I am weary and in need of
your strength. My body, mind, and spirit
are troubled, and I turn to you for
comfort and relief. Just as you healed
the sick and comforted the sorrowful,
please touch me with your healing hands

and restore me to health and peace.
Help me to bear my trials with patience
and trust in God's plan for me.

Our Lady of Good Health, you have been
a beacon of hope for those in distress. I
ask you to guide me through the
challenges I face, and grant me the
courage to persevere in faith. Teach me
to place my trust in God, and to find
solace in His love and mercy.

O Loving Mother, I pray for the grace to
accept God's will in my life, whether it
brings healing or continued suffering.
Help me to unite my pain with the
sufferings of Jesus, and to offer my trials
for the salvation of souls. Give me the
strength to endure with hope and joy,
knowing that your maternal care
surrounds me always.

Mary, Health of the Sick, be with me in
my moments of weakness and doubt.
Grant me the inner peace and serenity

that comes from knowing you are by my side. Help me to remain steadfast in prayer, and to trust that God hears my pleas and will answer them in His perfect time.

Thank you for hearing my prayer and for your unwavering love. With confidence, I place myself under your protective mantle, knowing that you will never abandon me.In your holy name, I pray. Amen.

Day 8

O Blessed Virgin Mary, Our Lady of
Good Health, I come before you today
with a heart full of faith and trust. You,
who have shown your loving care to
countless souls through miraculous
healings and answered prayers, I seek
your powerful intercession.

Mother of Mercy, I present my special
intention to you (mention your special
prayer request). You know the depth of
my need and the desires of my heart. In
your kindness and compassion, please
intercede for me with your Son, Jesus,
and ask Him to grant me the grace and
healing I so fervently seek.

O Mother, I am weary and in need of
your strength. My body, mind, and spirit
are troubled, and I turn to you for
comfort and relief. Just as you healed
the sick and comforted the sorrowful,

please touch me with your healing hands and restore me to health and peace. Help me to bear my trials with patience and trust in God's plan for me.

Our Lady of Good Health, you have been a beacon of hope for those in distress. I ask you to guide me through the challenges I face, and grant me the courage to persevere in faith. Teach me to place my trust in God, and to find solace in His love and mercy.

O Loving Mother, I pray for the grace to accept God's will in my life, whether it brings healing or continued suffering. Help me to unite my pain with the sufferings of Jesus, and to offer my trials for the salvation of souls. Give me the strength to endure with hope and joy, knowing that your maternal care surrounds me always.

Mary, Health of the Sick, be with me in my moments of weakness and doubt.

Grant me the inner peace and serenity that comes from knowing you are by my side. Help me to remain steadfast in prayer, and to trust that God hears my pleas and will answer them in His perfect time.

Thank you for hearing my prayer and for your unwavering love. With confidence, I place myself under your protective mantle, knowing that you will never abandon me.In your holy name, I pray. Amen.

Day 9

O Blessed Virgin Mary, Our Lady of Good Health, I come before you today with a heart full of faith and trust. You, who have shown your loving care to countless souls through miraculous healings and answered prayers, I seek your powerful intercession.

Mother of Mercy, I present my special intention to you (mention your special prayer request). You know the depth of my need and the desires of my heart. In your kindness and compassion, please intercede for me with your Son, Jesus, and ask Him to grant me the grace and healing I so fervently seek.

O Mother, I am weary and in need of your strength. My body, mind, and spirit are troubled, and I turn to you for comfort and relief. Just as you healed the sick and comforted the sorrowful, please touch me with your healing hands

and restore me to health and peace. Help me to bear my trials with patience and trust in God's plan for me.

Our Lady of Good Health, you have been a beacon of hope for those in distress. I ask you to guide me through the challenges I face, and grant me the courage to persevere in faith. Teach me to place my trust in God, and to find solace in His love and mercy.

O Loving Mother, I pray for the grace to accept God's will in my life, whether it brings healing or continued suffering. Help me to unite my pain with the sufferings of Jesus, and to offer my trials for the salvation of souls. Give me the strength to endure with hope and joy, knowing that your maternal care surrounds me always.

Mary, Health of the Sick, be with me in my moments of weakness and doubt. Grant me the inner peace and serenity

that comes from knowing you are by my side. Help me to remain steadfast in prayer, and to trust that God hears my pleas and will answer them in His perfect time.

Thank you for hearing my prayer and for your unwavering love. With confidence, I place myself under your protective mantle, knowing that you will never abandon me.In your holy name, I pray. Amen.

Nine-Day Meditation and Scripture Reading

Day 1: Trust in God's Plan

Reflection:
Today, let's reflect on the trust Mary had in God's plan. When the Angel Gabriel appeared to her, Mary responded with faith, despite not fully understanding God's will. In our own lives, we may face situations that confuse or challenge us. Like Mary, we are called to trust in God's plan, knowing that He is always working for our good.

Scripture Reading:
Luke 1:38
Mary said, "Behold, I am the servant of the Lord; let it be to me according to your word." And the angel departed from her.

Prayer:
Our Lady of Good Health, help me to trust in God's plan for my life. Even when I don't understand His ways, grant me the faith to say, "Let it be to me according to your word."

Day 2: Seeking Comfort in Times of Trouble

Reflection:
Mary, our Mother, experienced many hardships and sorrows, from the prophecy of Simeon to the crucifixion of her Son. Yet, she remained a source of comfort and strength for others. When we face our own troubles, we can turn to Mary, who understands our pain and offers us her maternal comfort.

Scripture Reading:
John 19:26-27
When Jesus saw his mother and the disciple whom he loved standing nearby, he said to his mother, "Woman, behold,

your son!" Then he said to the disciple, "Behold, your mother!" And from that hour the disciple took her to his own home.

Prayer:
Our Lady of Good Health, be my comfort in times of trouble. Help me to find strength in your love and to trust in your care.

Day 3: Embracing God's Healing

Reflection:
Throughout the Gospels, we see Jesus healing the sick and restoring health to the afflicted. Mary, as the mother of the Divine Healer, continues to intercede for us, bringing God's healing touch into our lives. Let us open our hearts to this healing, whether physical, emotional, or spiritual.

Scripture Reading:
Mark 5:34

And he said to her, "Daughter, your faith has made you well; go in peace, and be healed of your disease."

Prayer:
Our Lady of Good Health, intercede for me and bring God's healing into my life. Help me to have faith in His power to restore and renew.

Day 4: Strength in Suffering

Reflection:
Mary's life was marked by suffering, yet she endured with grace and strength. In our own suffering, we can find inspiration in her example. Let us ask for the grace to bear our crosses with courage and to unite our suffering with that of Christ.

Scripture Reading:
Romans 8:18
For I consider that the sufferings of this present time are not worth comparing

with the glory that is to be revealed to us.

Prayer:
Our Lady of Good Health, give me the strength to endure my suffering. Help me to offer it up to God, knowing that He can bring good out of every trial.

Day 5: Hope in the Face of Despair

Reflection:
Mary's hope never wavered, even in the darkest moments. Her faith and hope in God's promises sustained her. When we feel overwhelmed by despair, let us turn to Mary, who will help us to keep our eyes on the light of Christ.

Scripture Reading:
Jeremiah 29:11
For I know the plans I have for you, declares the Lord, plans for welfare and not for evil, to give you a future and a hope.

Prayer:
Our Lady of Good Health, instill in me a deep hope that does not waver. Help me to trust in God's promises and to remain hopeful, even in difficult times.

Day 6: Faithfulness in Prayer

Reflection:
Mary's life was a model of constant prayer and communion with God. She teaches us the importance of prayer in our own lives. Let us strive to deepen our prayer life, knowing that through prayer, we grow closer to God and receive His grace.

Scripture Reading:
Luke 1:46-47
And Mary said, "My soul magnifies the Lord, and my spirit rejoices in God my Savior."

Prayer:

Our Lady of Good Health, help me to be faithful in prayer. Teach me to make time for God each day and to seek His guidance and grace through heartfelt prayer.

Day 7: Love and Compassion for Others

Reflection:
Mary's life was marked by love and compassion for others. She visited Elizabeth to help her during her pregnancy and showed concern for the couple at the wedding in Cana. Let us ask Mary to help us grow in love and compassion, reaching out to those in need.

Scripture Reading:
John 2:3-5
When the wine ran out, the mother of Jesus said to him, "They have no wine." And Jesus said to her, "Woman, what does this have to do with me? My hour

has not yet come." His mother said to the servants, "Do whatever he tells you."

Prayer:
Our Lady of Good Health, inspire me to love and serve others with the same compassion you showed. Help me to be attentive to the needs of those around me and to respond with kindness and generosity.

Day 8: Peace in Our Hearts

Reflection:
Mary, Queen of Peace, shows us the way to true peace in our hearts. In a world filled with anxiety and unrest, we can find peace by turning to her and seeking her intercession. Let us ask Mary to help us cultivate inner peace and to share that peace with others.

Scripture Reading:
Philippians 4:6-7

Do not be anxious about anything, but in everything by prayer and supplication with thanksgiving let your requests be made known to God. And the peace of God, which surpasses all understanding, will guard your hearts and your minds in Christ Jesus.

Prayer:
Our Lady of Good Health, grant me peace in my heart. Help me to trust in God's love and to find rest in His presence. May your peace fill my soul and radiate to those around me.

Day 9: Gratitude for God's Blessings

Reflection:
Mary's Magnificat is a beautiful expression of gratitude for God's blessings. Let us end our novena by giving thanks for the many ways God has blessed us. Even in our struggles, there is always something to be grateful

for. Let us cultivate a spirit of gratitude, like Mary.

Scripture Reading:
Luke 1:49-50
For he who is mighty has done great things for me, and holy is his name. And his mercy is for those who fear him from generation to generation.

Prayer:
Our Lady of Good Health, I thank you for your loving intercession and for the many blessings God has bestowed upon me. Help me to always have a grateful heart and to recognize God's goodness in every aspect of my life. May my life be a testament to His love and mercy. Amen.

Made in the USA
Las Vegas, NV
07 January 2025

15970898R00042

9 798333 565259

CIALIS

Basic Guide On How To Boost Libido, Get Hard ,Stay Healthy , Stay Active Using Cialis

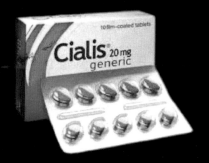

Dr. J. Christorph